FALLING TOWARD *the* MOON

**ALSO BY
ROBERT M. DRAKE**

Empty Bottles Full of Stories
with r.h. Sin

The King Is Dead

Dawn of Mayhem

Seeds of Wrath

Moon Matrix

The Great Artist

Dead Pop Art

Beautiful Chaos 2

Chaos Theory

Star Theory

Light Theory

Moon Theory

Beautiful and Damned

Gravity: A Novel

Seeds of Chaos

Beautiful Chaos

A Brilliant Madness

Black Butterfly

Broken Flowers

Spaceship

Science

also by r.h. Sin

Whiskey Words & a Shovel

Whiskey Words & a Shovel II

Whiskey Words & a Shovel III

Rest in the Mourning

A Beautiful Composition of Broken

Algedonic

She Felt Like Feeling Nothing

Planting Gardens in Graves

Planting Gardens in Graves Volume Two

Planting Gardens in Graves Volume Three

We Hope This Reaches You in Time
with Samantha King Holmes

Empty Bottles Full of Stories
with R. M. Drake

She Just Wants to Forget

ROBERT M. DRAKE

FALLING TOWARD *the* MOON

r.h. Sin

Cover illustration
by Hannah Olson

Andrews McMeel
PUBLISHING®

the FALLING

the **FALLING**
CONTENTS

WHY CHANGE	5
TEARING YOU UP	6
A MESSAGE ON FACEBOOK	8
PEACE IN	10
STILL HERE	13
A CALL FROM HEX	16
LIVE BY THIS, DIE BY THIS	18
WYNWOOD AGAIN	20
I WANT TO . . .	26
LEFT BEHIND	28
FLOWERS AGAIN	30
YOU DESERVE THIS	32
DO YOU SOME GOOD	33
THE . . .	36
CHASE THE STARS IN PEOPLE	37
AFTER TOMORROW	38

ENTIRE LIFE 40

ALMOST DELETED 44

BEAUTIFUL HUMAN 45

NEEDED MOST 47

SELF-LOVE 50

THE SHORELINE 53

DO NOT TAKE 54

NANCY 57

A LONG LIST 61

IMPORTANT CHOICES 64

SWEET GIRL 65

TIME LOSS 70

THE NEXT TIME 71

MISS YOU MISS THEM 74

FIGHT WARS 77

I COULD ALMOST 79

LAUGH IT OFF 85

NOTHING MORE OR LESS 87

MOODS 88

I WONDER ABOUT YOU 95

NOTICE YOU 96

SMART, STRONG, AND INTELLIGENT 98

SUPPOSED TO BE 100

LET IT 107

REGRETS 109

A TRIP THROUGH THE DAY 110

ALL IS GOOD 115

WHY CHANGE

You can't change people.

Assholes
are going to be
assholes.

Rebels
are going to be
rebels.

And loners
are going to be
loners, man.

But you can change
your perception of them.

And how all of them
don't want to be alone.

All of them need someone
or something

to love.

No matter what they say
or don't say.

the falling   5

TEARING YOU UP

I can tell something is
tearing you up inside.

Something terrible.

Something from your past
is haunting you

day in and day out.

I can see it in your sad eyes.
In your sad smile.

Something is hurting you
and it's eating you alive
without remorse.

Let it be known
that always in me,
you have a friend.

That always in me,
you have someone to talk to-

someone to listen
to what's aching your heart.

Let it be known
that whatever it is
you're going through . . .
it is something

you no longer
have to go through alone.

Let it be known,
my friend,

that I am here with you,

and I always have been,
and I will never leave your side

no matter how tragic
life gets.

A MESSAGE ON FACEBOOK

I get a DM.

One girl tells me
I am god.

That I always know
what she feels.

That my words
always come to her
at the right moment.

Soon after,
I get another DM.

Another girl tells me
that my work is trash

and that's all she writes
in the message.

I don't know what it is.

What I do.
Why I write.

Why I even read
their messages.

People are funny,
confused little creatures.

They either *love*
or *hate*

what they *don't understand.*

PEACE IN

You've got to work on yourself
day by day.

You've got to remember
that your entire life

is a work in progress.

That you're going to have
bad days but also good ones

to balance everything out.

You've got to know
that sometimes you're going to get
your heart broken.

While other times,
you're the one

who's going to be breaking
someone else's.

You've got to accept
that nothing ever goes as planned

and that *nothing* is perfect.
You've got to realize

that what you feel
is never wrong

and you must always trust
your intuition

but also accept
the consequence of things.

You've got to know
that it's never too late

to be where you want to be.

To become
who you want
to become.

To feel
what you want
to feel

and to love
the way you want
to be loved:

both freely
and without discrimination.

You've got to believe in this,
live by this,
and listen to your voice
when you have to.

In all shapes and forms.

You've got to empower
every human you love

and empower yourself
to be good
to those you don't love.

To be good, you know?

And let everything that brings
the light closer to you,

and everything
that brings you peace . . .

in.

STILL HERE

You're still here,
in this goddamn forsaken city.

And you're still walking,
breathing, and living,

no matter how much
it hurts inside.

You're still you.

You're still fighting,
trying to maintain-

waking up each day
and telling yourself

it's okay,
because it is.

You're still recovering.

You're still realizing your worth-
no matter how many times
you've been let down.

You're still here, goddammit!

Young and beautiful.

Full of pain
and full of laughter.

Cold and broken
but never alone.

The struggle is real.

You are real.
What you feel is real.

And you must realize your strength
and how you are capable of moving on.

You must realize the beauty
of finding yourself

and your natural ability to heal.

You must realize
how special you are,

and how you value yourself . . .
is the most important thing

in the world.

Always.

A CALL FROM HEX

The phone rang.

I woke up to get it
without knowing
what time is was.

"Goddamn fucking neighbors
have just woken me up."

It was my cousin, Hex.

He's been complaining
about his new neighbors
for the past two weeks.

"Can you fucking believe this?"

I stayed quiet
trying to focus my eyes.

"They've been waking me up
in the middle of the night . . .
with all their *fucking* noise."

I turned toward the clock
with the phone in my hands.

It said 4:21 a.m.

"Don't they fucking
know what time it is?

It's too late for this
type of shit.

Waking me up in the
middle of the night!"

He ranted, and never
did the exhaustion
find him.

I guess some people
don't notice what they do
until it's done to them.

While other people
will keep doing it

no matter who
tells them what.

LIVE BY THIS, DIE BY THIS

As long as I am with you,
I have nothing

to worry about.

Therefore,
the world could burn

and the birds can fall
from the sky.

I got you,
right now,

here in my arms
and we're surviving
through the destruction.

We are holding on
to what really matters,

to each other.

To our fears and desires.

I love that
because I need
that type of flame.
Flawed and in love.

We are alive
and there's nothing better

to live by
than that.

WYNWOOD AGAIN

Lost in a sunset.

In the lovely city
of Wynwood

I stand in the middle
of Wood Tavern
with a half-empty drink
in my hand.

The tunes flow . . .
they drip like honey
falling from the speakers.

The lights twinkle
fading in and out of the darkness.

I mind my business.

My comrades . . .

misunderstood,
angry,
and beaten.

They are worn
from the nine-to-five.

The sounds of music
are continuous . . .

they flow like the liquor
within the blood.

A brunette
friend of a friend
has found us in the crowd.

She walks over
swiftly,
flawlessly,
like a goddess
parting the sea.

She makes small talk
with a mutual comrade of ours.

I pay no attention.

Time passes by
and I caught her attention . . .

she asked for my name,

what I do,
and why I look so mad.

I am quiet.

Alone, here,
although my comrades
are with me

but, nonetheless, alone.

She asks me
why I am so serious . . .

if something was bothering me
and what was on my mind.

I tip the bartender,
ask for another drink,
and offer her one, too.

She asks for wine,
red wine.

I hate red wine.

I turn around,
pass her drink, and say,

"It's not that I'm mad.

The question is,
how could you not be,
with everything that's going on?

Anger is all I could feel.
The killings printed on paper.

The blood captured on video . . .
the mockery of life and death.

We entertain ourselves
with another man's tragic demise.

And then
we share it on social media
to pretend we care.

To say we need a change.

And we do,
but none of us want to take
that leap.

None of us want to risk
what we barely have.

Everyone is afraid,
waiting for someone

to do something about it,
anyone,
as long as it's not them.

And that's the problem here,"

I say as her face drops.

Of course,
that's the reaction I expected.

Of course,
I never planned to see her again.

She slowly stepped out of my frame
and I let her do so without hesitation.

Because I was too busy
thinking of this verse

when I got home

and she was too busy
pretending

she was listening
to what I said.

I WANT TO . . .

I want you to feel-
to remember what it was like

when you first laid eyes on
something you loved.

I want you to breathe,
to inhale.

To run your fingers
through the air

and collect the memories
as they pass you by.

I want you to remember

the way we spoke.

The way we looked
into our eyes
as the scent filled

the empty
space in the room.

I want you to feel it.
To remember it.
To be
attracted to it.

I want the company
of me

to remind you

how to live,
how to laugh,

and, above all,
how to love.

LEFT BEHIND

I look far away
and remember what
you left behind.

I remember the ocean breeze.

The waves
and the falling
of rain.

With deep breaths
and steady thoughts.

The heart skips
and never desires
to slip away.

You hold me
and with one slow inhale
I am taken back-

I am reminded of everyone
I have ever loved,

of everything
I have ever wanted.

Your fragrance has me.
It pulls me in and out
of my past, my future.

And the moment
you're gone
my night is never the same.

In all rawness
and love . . .

what I'm trying to say is,

even after we part,
your scent pushes me
toward the light . . .

lost,
drunk in love,

and lingering
in a place

where only
the flowers
can grow.

FLOWERS AGAIN

This is about the flowers
and the way
the wind blows the petals
as they fall.

This is about the rain
and the sound it makes
as it hits the window.

This is about
the last car ride home

and the way it makes you
reminisce about all the
places you miss.

This is about laughter
and the way it triggers feelings

you once had
as a child.

This is about people
and the way

their hands hold on to one another
without knowing
when to let go.

This is about love . . .

the way two people
find one another

and the way they
lose themselves in

a garden full of roses.

This is about you.

About your life.

About the way you look,
the way you feel,

and

the way your scent fills
the room.

YOU DESERVE THIS

The way you need
to be loved

and the way you want
are two very different things.

One you can learn
to live without

while the other
will take a lifetime
to accept.

You have to listen to yourself,
to what you need,
feel,

to be willing
to lose yourself in

the kind of love
you deserve.

DO YOU SOME GOOD

I hope you find someone
who's real with you.

Someone who's capable
of telling you
when you're wrong,

when you're about
to make a mistake.

I hope you find someone
who's not afraid to love.

Someone who's not afraid
to get hurt.

I hope you find more
than just a lover.

I hope you find a friend,
and I hope they love you,
really love you,

and I hope they love
themselves as well.

I hope you find someone
who cares—
not just someone
who cares about you

but also someone
who cares about others.

Someone who cares
about making a difference,

about leaving
some kind of mark
on the world:

to heal it,
change it for the best.

In the most genuine way,
I hope someone like this
finds you,

whether you're searching for them
or not.

Because there are so many reasons
for you to be happy.

So many chances
to let go of everything
that brings you down.

I hope you let
"being in love"

with the right person
be a small part

of something

that's meant
to do you
some good.

THE . . .

The birds fly.
The leaves fall.

The seasons change.
The wind causes friction
on my skin.

The sun rotates.

It hides.
It appears.

It shines
no matter what.

The oceans feel ease.
The waves flow,
and most of the time,

I am here,

thinking

about you.

CHASE THE STARS IN PEOPLE

Kid,
I gave you
what you asked for.

What you wanted.

I gave you my heart
and you had it.

Sadly,
you let it slip away.

Some people chase something
their entire lives,

and when they finally find it,
they lose it.

They regret it

and realize
what they've lost

as soon as it's
gone.

AFTER TOMORROW

After tomorrow,
a new year starts.

After tomorrow,
a new opportunity arises.

After tomorrow,
a new version of you
is born.

Take what you've learned
this year and heal from it.

Grow from it.

And understand
how beautiful it is
to reach this point-

to stand and inhale
the life you've been granted.

Let this new year
be *your* year.

Let it be the second chance
you've been wanting to take.
Let it be
the answers
you've been looking for.

Let this New Year
consume you.

Let it guide you.

And let it give you
the hope you need

to move forward.

After tomorrow,
it begins,

and you must know
how only the best

is yet to come.

ENTIRE LIFE

You spend your whole life
worrying about being alone,

that you've let
so many good people
pass you by.

The same way you've spent
so much time
thinking of those who don't care

rather than the ones
who do.

And this is what your life
has turned into.

Chasing people
who don't understand you

while overlooking

the ones who relate
to you the most.

You've let so much
time slip,

you've let too many
people slip,

and now you're slipping yourself . . .

by chasing people
who've caused you the most harm.

When does it end?

When do you finally realize
who you are?

Whom you deserve?
Does it ever stop?

The pain.
The brokenness.

The emptiness
and the longing of being
understood-of being

held by the right hands.

I get you.

You feel like the ocean—
the rain—

but that doesn't mean
you've got to drown on your own.

With water comes life.
And with pain comes love.

So hang in there,
my sweet friend . . .

life isn't meant
to destroy you.

People aren't meant
to hurt you . . .

and all the things you feel
aren't meant to bring you closer

to your doom.

Because everything around you
is a lesson waiting to be learned,

and how you let it
affect you

is completely up to you.

So cry now and laugh later . . .
it's okay . . .

because something better
is on the way.

Just stay humble,
learn from your mistakes,

and keep your heart open
for when the right

opportunities come.

ALMOST DELETED

A girl sends me
a message on Instagram.

She says,

"Where do you get
your inspiration?"

I reply.

"Life, my dear, life."

My laughter.
My sweat.
My tears.

My pain.
My love.
My loss.

My gain.
My experience.
And my writing.

Will always

be based on
life.

ROBERT M. DRAKE   44

BEAUTIFUL HUMAN

Beautiful human beings
come and go.

So there is no reason
to believe they were
the one.

You're going to think that
about everyone
you fall in love with.

You're going to believe
that's "the one" each time.

And then,
this is how it usually happens.

Like five years pass
and, suddenly,

you open your eyes
for the first time.

You find yourself laughing
a little harder.

Holding hands
a little tighter
and growing with one person
for the past few years.

And for reasons unknown,
it always feels
as if

time has flown by
far too quickly.

You spend several years
with someone

and by the time you know it-

it's been a lifetime.

That's how it works.

You never quite find love.
It finds you

and reveals itself
when you least expect it to.

All the time.

ROBERT M. DRAKE   46

NEEDED MOST

That's expected of you.

To look for help,

for someone to pour yourself out to
when you need it most.

Because no one
wants to deal

with heart-shattering things
on their own.

Human beings are social creatures

and everyone needs someone
to feel them.

To sit down and talk.
To share a cup of coffee with

and explore themselves.

So ask for help.

Seek it.

I advise you to.
Complete solitude should never
be an option,
because you have plenty

of people
who genuinely care.

People who feel
the same way,

who are currently going
through moments

just as bad as you are.

All you have to do
is overcome the fear

of being judged
and overcome yourself

for what you feel.

Everything else
will always fall

into place.

Just remember

to give yourself
to people with an open heart.

To say what's on your mind
and to never isolate yourself

from people
when *you* need them most.

SELF-LOVE

Self-love is about survival.

About finding your own
path and passing through.

It's not about
the opinions of others.

It's not about
holding on to the things
that bring you harm—

to the things
that hurt.

It's not about
forgetting who you are—

what you want
and need.

No, never that.

In detail,
it's about you.

About watering your own soul
the best way
you know how.

It's about finding
your own truth–

about knowing
what kind of love
you deserve.

And it's something
that can't be taught
but earned.

It's something
that's not given freely

but obtained through experience
and struggle.

And it's not easy.

It's one of the hardest things
to do, let alone practice.

But once you know it.

Once you finally accept yourself
for who you are,

then
it becomes
somewhat of a miracle.

It becomes a blessing,
and it is one

only you can give
to yourself.

So this I tell you,

in all truth and rawness.

Life is too short
not to love yourself,

and in some sense,
you deserve to find
your perfect happiness,

no matter what kind
of lies

you've been told.

ROBERT M. DRAKE 52

THE SHORELINE

Sometimes,

you feel like you've spent
your whole life

planning

for a future that isn't certain.

Chasing a love
that doesn't exist.

And worrying about
a past that doesn't even matter.

And this is what your life
has turned into.

Stressing over the unknown.
Overthinking about people
you've never even met

and dwelling in moments
that drown you,

instead of the ones
that push you
toward the shore.

DO NOT TAKE

Don't take yourself
too seriously.

Don't spend your days
working too hard

and don't spend your nights
overthinking
the future.

Don't mistreat people
and don't pretend

to be

something you're not.

Don't judge others
based on your own life

and don't hold on
when there's nothing left

to hold on to.

Don't wait
if you're not expecting
and don't think you know
when you really don't.

Don't laugh
if you don't want to

and don't take people
for granted.

So many don'ts
in this list, some obvious, too.

But the problem is

you know what's wrong
and, still,

there will be times
you will ignore it.

And you will follow
your heart

even if it means harm.

That's human life.

We experience tragedies
and sometimes it's our own fault.

And sometimes,
we can't control
the outcome—

sometimes,

we'll do what's wrong
because we'll feel

as if

it's the right thing
to do.

The fire burns,
and our hands have scars,

and we'll lean over
because we want to.

Every. Single. Time.

NANCY

Nancy, a young brunette,

a friend of mine for many years.

She only calls me
when she needs me.

When she feels alone.

Most of the time
she rants about the man
she is currently seeing.

She says how much
he doesn't appreciate her.

How much
he takes everything she does
for him for granted.

Of course
there is another side
to the story.

And if you've ever been
on the side
that gives the advice,

you know how people
never tend to talk about
their faults in the situation.

They just pick at the person
they're complaining about

and ignore
the cause of their troubles.

Nancy,
being Nancy,

a smart, witty girl
with a little darkness,

and what she doesn't say is . . .

how she pushes people away.

She has this terrible
little temper.

This little tick, a silent rage.

She looks into everything.
She is paranoid and believes

everyone she is with
is bound to be her doom.

In other words,
she doesn't trust anyone.

No matter how long
she's been with them.

It's always the same story.

"No one cares,"
she says, over the phone.

"Everyone is all the same."

My dear,
when will you learn?

That it is not that you can't
trust anyone.

It is more
that you cannot trust
yourself.

She doesn't let people in
unless it's her way

and then she wonders
why no one ever takes

the time
to try to save her.
Why no one ever seems
to care enough.

Or love her
the way she needs
to be loved.

And it is easy to point out.

That she is
how she is

because she has not
only failed to understand

but also

failed
to love herself.

A LONG LIST

I have a long list
of people I've done wrong,

of people
I've tried to love
but have failed.

And I'm not proud of it.

I don't take credit
for breaking people's hearts.

For falling in love with them—
to suddenly leave them behind.

The thing is,

and maybe I'm the only person
who feels this way,

but I don't know
who I am at times.

I don't know
what to feel—what to say
or think.

I could wake up one day
and be totally in love with something,

with you,

and then the next day
wake up

wanting to be left alone-isolated,

somewhere in some place
that has yet to be discovered.

This is the way
my heart works

and I've learned this.

I'm trying to adapt
to the way I change.

Because some nights,
I feel like I'm on top of the world

while other nights
I feel like I'm buried beneath it.

And this is what
depression feels like.

Like I'm two different people
and both of them

barely know who they are.

They sit alone at a table
and they barely

understand themselves.

IMPORTANT CHOICES

There comes a time
when you must make
a choice.

And I don't mean
one of those silly little choices

between what shoes to wear
or pants to put on.

I mean
the kind of choice

that is going to change
your life forever.

Because bad things are going to happen
and some good things too

but it's how you let them
affect you.

That within itself
is the most important choice
of them all.

SWEET GIRL

My sweet girl,
I see you now running across
the living room.

Laughing without a clue
of how hard this life is going
to be for you.

It almost hurts me.

The fact that at this moment
you believe your world

is perfect,
and it is,

that is, for what it is.

You're still a little girl.

You have so much
to grow into.

So much room to fill.
So much pain to go through.

So much suffering
you'll never expect
to happen.

My sweet girl.
My sweet little girl.

In all your glory
you're running across
without a care.

If there is anything I can do,

anything you can remember
whenever you feel the aches

of your heart or
the tears flowing from your eyes

or the intensity
you will carry within your
bones.

If there is anything
I can do,

it is to tell you
that all things pass.

That all pain eventually
dissolves.

That time heals everything
and what it doesn't

you have to step away from
and learn to heal
on your own.

My sweet girl.

With every fiber in your body,
every atom,
and every connection . . .

know

that, yes,
life is hard.

Losing people is hard.
Losing opportunities is hard.

Losing love is hard.

But losing yourself
in what hurts
is even harder.

Just believe
that somewhere within you

there is a special kind
of light.
It is the kind
that can overcome

any kind
of darkness.

All you have to do
is close your eyes
and remember . . .

what it was like
when you were just
a little girl

because
that will always

represent
the best parts of me

and also

the best parts
of you.

TIME LOSS

The first half
of your life

you'll spend
acquiring wealth

and social status.

And the second half
of your life

you'll spend learning
how the first half

of your life
really meant nothing
at all.

THE NEXT TIME

Do not become
one of those people

who become dependent
on the person they love.

You know,
that kind of person

who once they feel
as if they've found someone,

they ignore
everyone who's been there
for them.

Do not become this person.

Do not forget the people
you have around you.

Do not ignore them
because for the time being

you feel as if
you have the one
you need.

Do not become this type of person.

No one wants to be
this person

but almost too often
do they become it.

So please,
for Christ's sake,

the next time you find yourself
in a hot pile of love,

do not detach yourself
from your friends.

From your family.
From the people who really care.

Because lovers come and go.

Some hurt you
and some heal you

but those who've watched you grow
are something else.

It is something
you can't put into words.

It is something you just feel,
you know?

So, please,
do not become this person.

You owe it to the people
who care

to be so much more
than that.

I hope you take this with you.

Now good-bye.

MISS YOU MISS THEM

People will miss you
the moment you stop caring.

The moment you moved on.
Because that's how it works.

Most people only want
what no longer belongs to them,

what they once had
but failed to appreciate.

And it's sad,
you know?

Because you can spend
so much time devoted

to someone
while feeling ignored,

but the moment you realize
your worth,
things begin to change.

ROBERT M. DRAKE 74

You begin to do things
for yourself.

You begin to see the light,
feel it, and become it.

You move on to bigger
and better things.

You meet different people
and for a moment

you find yourself being happy.

And it's just sad
but also very good

because you had to let go
of someone who was once

important to you
to find yourself again.

You had to water your own soul
and find your own smile.

And you spent
and wasted so much time
doing so,

without knowing
how to love yourself before.

And that's what's terrible here.
That's the tragedy.

How you always need someone
to help you discover your worth

and how you always need
to lose someone you once cared about.

Need someone
you once loved

to dig a hole in you,
in order for you to finally

learn to appreciate yourself
for who you are.

FIGHT WARS

We fight their wars.

We come home
and they give us a statue.

We die for what they believe in.

We come home
and they give us a medal.

They praise us for our bravery . . .
for how we fought each night.

And then
we come back home.

They take away our businesses.
They take away our culture.
They take away our pride and legacy.

And then
they wonder why none of us
truly succeed.

Not unless we work for them.
Not unless we join their revolution.

One built on blood,
sweat, tears, and sacrifice.

We fight their wars,
my love,
my people,

because if we do not,
we are thrown
to the wolves,

in jail to rot.

And then
some of us don't even make it
back home.

No,
instead,

we come back
in a box full of medals

and maybe,
if we are lucky,

we get a statue
with our name.

ROBERT M. DRAKE   78

I COULD ALMOST

I could almost feel
my heart beating.

I am not dead yet.

There's still a fight in me-
a will I cannot describe.

If anything I have done
has been meaningful

throughout the years,
writing has got to be it.

The dark room
swallows the walls.

The bed, the headboard,
and the ceilings.

Writing.

It has got to be
all for the art.

For the words
that I do not know enough.

The plasma screen blinks.

Bright,
out the window

the street lamp flickers.

All is calm, quiet.

All except
what lies beneath my chest,
behind my eyes.

I could now feel it,
my heart.

Alive and well.

Strong yet weak
and fragile.

Welcoming to all things
that shatter.

Relating to it.

Picking out the similarities
and saying, you're like me.

You're not alone.

Although,
we are not the same.

I lie here.

Listening to the air conditioner.
Listening to the loud sounds
that dwell deep within my ears.

The om.

The humming of life
and death.

The never-ending beep
that surfaces only when no one
is around.

I write more.

These words.

As if I feel
even more confused
than ever.

As the paranoia kicks in.

I am not alone.

No one understands.
They never do,
although they want to.

Perhaps it is me,
and I am not clear enough.

But none of that matters.

Nothing ever does
unless it affects your life.

I mean,
it really has to change it.

Other than that,
it is all a shot in the dark.

You know,
a shot within a shot.

Who knows.

But I'm still here . . .

for reasons unknown
but the words . . .

my incoherent thoughts.

The loss of one's mind.

I am forgetting
and it all feels like a dream.

All things,
most things,

gone

like a year-old love letter.

Ignored and uncared for.

This is me.

My words are me
and it either makes sense to you
or not.

But like I said,
none of it matters.

It does only
if it means something

and if it changes your life
for good.

LAUGH IT OFF

Now imagine that,
all the bridges I had to burn.

All the people
I had to leave behind.

All the times
I had to say good-bye . . .

the times I had
to reinvent myself

and the times
I had to tell myself
to keep going.

Now imagine this,

all the bridges
I had to rebuild.

All the people
I had to chase.

All the times
I said hello . . .

the times
I broke down
and the times

I found more.

I hope one day
we find each other again
and laugh

over whatever pain
we might have caused.

NOTHING MORE OR LESS

When it's time for you
to love,

you're going to love.

The same way
when it's time for you to hurt,

you're going to hurt.

Your life
is perfectly balanced.

You will hurt
and love
when it is necessary.

Nothing more.
Nothing less.

MOODS

I go through moods
when I love people

and then
I go through moments

when I wish
I was the last person
alive,

when I wish
I was a legend.

And this is one
of those times,
the bad times.

When I was in high school,
I wasn't outspoken.

I wasn't the popular guy.
In fact,

for reasons unknown
I managed to be barely

noticeable.

ROBERT M. DRAKE   88

I always kept low
and only kept a few

good comrades
around me.

We did graffiti.
We made music.
We drank beers.
We fought.

We got in trouble
with the cops.

Hell,
we even went
to jail a few times.

The chaos of my adolescence.

After all of that,
still,
nobody cared.

Growing up
nobody cared,

not unless you had
something they wanted,
and most of the time

it was about image,
about being cool,
looking cool.

You know,
things that have
no true force.

Things that are illusions.
Things that do not matter.

It was only then,
when I began college,

that people began
to notice me

for my art,
for my ability
to sculpt and paint.

They came in herds
asking for help
and I gave it

every time.

Soon after,
when I graduated,
no one seemed to come around.

Not until
I began to work

at Univision
as an art director.

That's when
they came for me again,
for help,

for anything
I could do
to get them a gig
at the network.

When I left Univision,
soon after,

they disappeared again,
and it wasn't until

my writing situation
took off on social media

when the oceans of people
returned.

They returned for something,
for help,
for a piece of what I built.

Whether it was
help building their brand,
money, or fame.

*They never stopped
coming for more.*

People I hadn't spoken to
in years appeared,
and people I didn't even know

out of the blue
wanted to *"help me"*

and everything for *"me."*
But in the end,

it was always for
their own personal gain.

I got smarter.
I got colder.

And now
I understand why
some of the most successful people

suffer from depression
and why they feel
most alone.

It's a never-ending love song.

People will always be looking
for an easy way out,
and they will use you,

take everything from you
while you're not looking,

and forget you
the moment they take
what you have.

Their interest,
like a thirst,

and once they start
it's very hard
to run away from.

They are wolves
in sheep's clothing

but I have always been
a lion trapped

in an unlocked cage.

AMEN.

I WONDER ABOUT YOU

You can break
all of me

but for
Christ's sake

do not touch
my hands.

Let them be,
for I need them

to hold you
through the night.

I need them
to keep you company

whenever you
feel

like running away
from it all.

NOTICE YOU

I have this feeling
that you want me

to believe
that you're broken,

that you're this miserable,
lonely person.

This human being
who endures

all types of hurting,
right?

But I think you're wrong.
I know deep down

within you,
within that hurting body,
there's more

and it's something
beyond what the eye could see.

And I know
it's ferocious.

It doesn't contain fear.

You're strong
but that doesn't mean
you have to be alone.

People love you,
so you should *let them*
love you.

People will always notice you
for who you really are.

SMART, STRONG, AND INTELLIGENT

I knew I loved her
because she loved life.

She cared for it
as if any moment

she might slip away.

To where?

That's something
I'll never know

but it's not like
it mattered . . .

for whether she stayed
or left me behind,

I'd still love her.

I'd still need her,
want her,

and it would be
the same way

any other man
would want his woman.

Smart,
strong,
and intelligent.

Never weak
and too beautiful
to ignore.

SUPPOSED TO BE

Of course,
you feel like
you can't trust her.

I mean,
a woman like that
is surreal,
like a dream.

With fierce eyes
as if she were made up

in the minds
of a hundred mad men.

She's *too much*
to handle,

too much woman
for the average man.

One minute
she's the center of a storm,
calm and collected,

and then
the next second
she's walking on the edge
of chaos,

the sun,
and where all things go

to dissolve into
thin air.

You inhale,
grasp for what is not there.

And, sure,
she makes you feel

uncomfortable.

She's supposed to
do that.

She's supposed to
make you feel as if

you're not sure
about anything,

not this world
or the next.

Not life or death.
Not love or loneliness.

And now
since there is
nothing for you,

nothing to rely on . . .
you leave,

walk out on the things
that scare you.

Things that put
the fear of the unknown
before you . . .

but

before you go
and release her
into the wild,

where she came from,
where she might forget
who you are.

Always remember

how the two of you
are not the same.

How you may think
you understand her,

know her,
and feel her

because you've spent
a few nights with her . . .

but you don't.

In fact,
you know nothing
of her
as many men do.

And remember this:
she's a wild card

and just because
you can't handle her

doesn't mean
she wants you to
in the first place.

She's more,
more than you could
break down.

She's the core
of what moves,

the heat that slowly
converts all the people

she loves
into clouds.

ROBERT M. DRAKE   104

She's the maker
of dreams,

the inspiration
that's needed to change

the dark to light.

She's the complex
drift of the moon

and the gentle pull
of the tide.

Goddammit,
men like you
fear perfection.

And that's why
you don't understand her,
and it's okay
if you don't,

but, please,
for the love you haven't
tasted,

don't destroy her.

For she's a flower,
so if you want nothing

with her,
then by all means,

let her bloom,
let her roam,

freely,

and let her be.

LET IT

You can't stop love.

You can't beat it either
but *it can* beat the oxygen
out of your body.

And it is strong enough
to kill you,
to destroy an entire building
without the use of bombs.

You can't stop love–
that is never
going to happen,
the same way you can't stop
death or birth

or laughter
or pain
or all the things
that rush toward your life

for better or worse.

You can't stop love,
so let it happen.

Let it give you all the stupid
little reasons to do it,
to find it.

You can't stop love.
You can't stop anything
from happening . . .

so let it.

Let it.
Let it . . .

all consume
you.

REGRETS

Sometimes
it feels like I am moving
backward

and sometimes
the past is all I have
to remind me

that I should have
loved you

a little harder.

A TRIP THROUGH THE DAY

When I saw
the love of my life
pass by.

It was the first
day of class
and I was in my third
semester in college.

I was taking
a time base media course
and I was waiting outside
of the classroom,

that is,
waiting for the professor
to arrive.

While I was waiting,
I saw my breath flow
out of me
to mock me
and tease me
over my own words.

Then a goddess
with long swaying hair,
big sad eyes,
and mouthful of glitter
as if she had tasted
the night sky . . .

caught my attention
from afar.

Of course
my heart was on my sleeve.
My eyes were looking
at the dirt
and my soul
far off to some distant place.

We spoke briefly.
She was looking for her class.

Soon enough she had to go
and she went off
into the buildings

into the backdrop
like a wild fox
running out of a
burning forest.

That was five years ago.

Now
instead of remembering
her skin,
her eyes,
her lips and hair,

all I could remember
was what I last
said to her
the very last moment
we shared.

"I hope I see you around."

I never saw her again,
although
I wish I had.

It was just
that
something inside of me
wished I had said
something better,
something worthwhile,

something that would make her
remember me.

Now the reason
I'm here,
writing this down,

is this . . . .
about a month ago,
I ran into her,
and once again,
she was gone.

I watched her pass by me
without exchanging
a single word.

And to think,
there goes
the love of my life,
perhaps.

A woman
I could have loved.

A woman
I could have
grown old with.

A woman
who could have known
all of my secrets.

But in the end,
she's just another woman
I never had
the courage to meet.

Another *"what if"*
lost in the thread of time.

ALL IS GOOD

The only thing
wrong with our love

is the
way we exceed
to love others

but barely had enough

to love
ourselves.

the landing

it begins I.

I have this pretty awful feeling bubbling beneath
the surface of my mind. I've been overthinking
myself closer to a version of hell that consists of
me staying up odd and lonely hours of the night.
Fighting for my sanity, searching for my peace.
Unable to find myself and everything I lost,
the moment I allowed myself to think of you as
something more than you should've been. I could
be sleeping right now but instead I have this
awful thought of you thinking of someone else
other than me. Sometimes I wish I was on your
mind as much as you destroy mine.

it rarely ends.

I sit quietly with only the sound of my soul
weeping an internal sadness. I'm breaking
beneath this smile, dying in the silence of my
own heartache. Where do tears go when they're
not visible? Where does the strength go when the
heart feels weak? I'd speak but I can't find the
words. I want to scream but I can't find my voice.

overcome, again.

Your heart the size of the moon, creating its own
light, and even though you feel broken, you still
continue to fight. No weapons, no shield, just
a will to survive. You feel weary beneath the
sadness and yet you still try.

muscle memory.

I can recall being exactly where you were,
feeling exactly the way you felt. The days
usually become slower than usual. The mornings
are tough, and by afternoon, you almost feel
as though giving up or giving in is your only
option. The evenings are just as difficult as
you struggle to capture moments of delight and
peace. I've been exactly where you were in those
moments of light denial during your darkest
times. Searching for the type of light that could
chase away the shades of gray consuming spaces
where happiness used to exist. I know what it
means to live a life that resembles a plant that is
slowly dying or holding on to hope during the
most hopeless of moments. That sort of pain
resonates with me in the most profound way; that
sort of chaos was once the most familiar thing I'd
known.

I wrote this to let you know that you are not
alone. It may feel like you're the only one
struggling through life or it may feel like you're
the only one who knows heartache just as well as
you know yourself, but we've all been there and
some of us are still there. Trying to stay afloat on
the deep end of everything but I honestly believe
that there's hope, there's a shift.

There's a change that can happen, but in order to get there, you must continue to overcome the troubles that exist here on this earth, in your life. You must continue to walk even when you believe that your feet won't manage. You must continue to fight even when your knuckles are busted, and you must continue to love yourself even when others refuse to.

Within you lives this ability to overcome any obstacle. Within you lives this strength to overcome and push against and push through the negatives that stand before you. Within you lives this magic that most people will never understand, and that's okay because only you need to comprehend it. Harness that energy, cultivate and maintain that power because it will be you that will save you. It has always been you that has saved you, and if you've done it before, you can do it again. You are not alone.

it begins II.

It's 11 at night; the midnight moon sits in the distance. Whispering outside my window while my eyes remain fixated on the ceiling and my mind drifts off into a cluster of ideas and thoughts that seem to always be centered around you. I run circles around us each night and yet no amount of movement has gotten me close enough to figure out what this actually is. I sit up for a moment, my eyes in search of stars like my heart in search of answers, but I draw blanks like a pen without ink, pressed firmly against hemp paper.

The later it gets, the deeper I dwell in an unforgiving pit of confusion. Maybe I'm in love with an illusion. Maybe I hold on to the idea of holding on to you out of fear of losing. Strangely, it's the loss of something I never had that keeps me hoping for something you'll never give me. And each night I'm right where I left off come morning. Somehow I find myself back where I began. A start with no actual finish. This never-ending feeling for something that should have ended a long time ago. It turns out that I've been searching for a silver lining in a bronze space.

I've been searching for some sort of light in a sky that is absent of the sun, and yeah, of course, the moon is out, but I believe I need more than what these evenings usually provide. I need more time for me instead of wasting these moments on trying to figure out what I mean to your life. I need more sleep and less of you.

what will happen.

There will be men who never show up but will claim to miss you. There will be men who claim to love you while treating you like shit. There will be men who tell lies and yet expect you to believe them. There will be men who betray you and yet they'll still expect you to trust them. There will be men who say all the right things but their actions will never match what they speak. There will be men who claim to be sorry then continue to do the things they're always apologizing for. There will be men who won't claim you but expect you to bear their child. There will be men who will fall short in every area you need them to excel in. There will be men who will make you hate the fact that you care about them. These men were never worth it. These men are never worth it. These men don't deserve your energy. These men no longer deserve your attention. Stay away from these types of men. Walk away from these types of men.

There will be men who are nothing but lessons and examples of what to avoid as you move forward with your life, and once you move forward with your life, avoid these types of men as much as you can. There is love, an honest love. A deep love, the type of love that provides peace. There is a love that will outlast the pain and overshadow all of the aches in your heart, but in order to find it, you have to practice letting go of those who are content with letting you down. These men, the men described in this passage, will serve as stepping-stones to someone who is better than all of them.

you spend all your life looking for love

and it's only when you get to the end

that you realize that you forgot

to look for yourself

and that is the saddest love story

of them all

journeying through life

beside a lover who can't love you

is like building a home on land

overtaken by drought

in love alone in the valley of death

in Manhattan.

There's this gentle sigh of sadness that walks the
streets of New York City at night. The lights in
Times Square create this illusion of excitement
while hiding this underlying sense of pain. Look
closely at the people all dressed up, filling dark
rooms with other people who are wearing the
same masks. They're all running from something,
and just for a moment, the loud music and alcohol
help them get away. This city is beautiful, but its
occupants are often feeling the ugliest of things,
and instead of facing their truth, they'd rather
pretend, but I see through their New York smog.
I hear their anguish over the crowds of tourists.
I bump into strangers all the time, and it's like
I feel what has been hidden for far too long.
Manhattan, I see your truths.

far and near.

midnight moon
in May, dreaming of June
soon this will be over
soon i will be sober

free of these chains
no longer bound by
the time i invested
in a love
that never manifested

you were the nothing
i should've ignored
you were the something
i should've stayed away from

and so i sit
beneath a midnight moon
thinking soon
i'll walk away from you

maybe she was tired
of being told how beautiful
she was

maybe all she wanted
was to be treated
like she mattered

Selene.

Moon child, the sun is fading away. This is your
moment.

corners.

we live in a corner

our backs pressed against the wall

afraid of moving forward

afraid of letting go

afraid of starting over

with something or someone new

and so we stay there in that corner

that small cramped space

that keeps us from getting the things

we crave the most

because real love and truth and joy

can only be found when searched for

but in order to find them

we must learn to leave that corner

we must learn to walk ahead

_____

that overpowering desire

to stay in a relationship

with someone who refuses

to give you what you desire most

is a version of hell

that seems to be a struggle

to get away from

————————

i can't sleep

it's almost as if

the night needs me more

than i need rest

my dreams are in black and white

my nightmares are blind

no picture

just the sound of you

telling me lies

the pictures capture the lies so well

painting smiles on sad faces

＿＿＿＿＿＿＿＿

the bombs are dropping in my heart

but they're all silent

and so i'll smile

to keep them from knowing

how it really feels to feel like me

_____

a long life

is a slow death

you find yourself

fighting to survive

and the longer you live

the closer you are to the end

please.

most of the love
i knew before you
were tragedies
wrapped in good intent
and lies that sounded so beautiful
they had to be true

i was guilty of showering lovers
with things they never deserved
fooled, used, and confused
by empty promises

i gave and got nothing
but bruises, scars,
and the inability to sleep

i began to drink more often

abusing myself with different elixirs

with the intent of forgetting

and so i'm sorry if it takes me longer

to receive you in a way

that makes you comfortable

i wish i could fall freely

but i've done that before

only to find myself landing

on a bed of rusty nails

with apologies for band-aids

but rarely did they ever help

so please forgive me

my hesitance is a remnant

of all the times i've been hurt

by anyone claiming to love me

———————————

no one knows

what lives beneath this smile

no one ever hears

the sadness in my laughter

————————

you feel broken

you feel sadness

you feel pain

but you are not less

———————

sometimes i avoid mirrors

because a reflection never lies

the mirror doesn't concern itself

with showing you something that isn't true

it has no concern for how you feel

it knows your insecurities

and it doesn't mind throwing them back at you

time wasted.

and that's the problem
thinking we have more time
than we actually do

wasting ourselves on lovers
who could never love us
the way we wish

giving away our firsts
without concern
of what we'll have left

trying for people
who refuse to make an effort
giving our best selves
to the worst relationships

and one day we wake up
at the tail end of our lives
wishing for more time
a request that is often denied

all that was left

were sharp-edged moments

cutting at my mind

splitting my soul

and breaking my heart

we were nothing but memories

of everything i wished to forget

i too shatter easily

i'm just good

at pretending to be okay

just like you

mber.

my head lately

...n the past and whatever is left

of memories of you

i've been living in my head
running away from reality
reconstructing memories of us
painting lies of who we were
i've been stretching your truths
pretending to have remembered
myself happier than i actually was

the memories of what could have been
will haunt me as i struggle to sleep
and you will be my everlasting nightmare
your ghost will leave me restless

there are nights where i shout prayers

to an empty sky in hopes

of drowning out the voices in my head

the deafening noises of depression

it's dreary hands reaching for my throat

where midnight feels suffocating

and the silence is loud

_____

her hands could hold a hurricane

her touch could calm the sea

_____

but darling

you will never matter

to a fool who doesn't

deserve you

she moved like the flame
on top of a wick of a candle
with flashes of magic
in her hips

she's a flame
not the kind you flee from

her fire is the torch
that can set you free

her fire is the light
that will guide you
if you love her enough

—————————

sometimes i wish the heart
could see more and feel less

maybe then it would be easier
to let go of people who no longer
deserve its love

_____

starting over

will be one of the hardest things

you'll ever have to do

but nothing is worse

than pretending to be happy

in a relationship

that drowns your heart

losing a queen.

don't you get it yet?
her heart was not an object
to be used or broken

her heart was your best chance
at a future of devotion and joy

that heart will be
your greatest loss
her heart will always be
the very thing
you never deserved

and once you lose her
she'll learn to survive
in a world
that no longer
consists of being hurt by you

September 1st 2018.

Any man who chooses to neglect your heart is
replaceable. Any man who decides to be disloyal
to you is not worthy of your devotion. Do not
give weak men the license to operate in your
life because you are meant for something more.
You are meant for someone who is capable of
giving you everything you give. I hope you
find the courage to start choosing yourself
rather than holding on to the person who has
chosen everything else and everyone else over
you. I know it's been difficult as of late, you're
constantly battling yourself and this idea of
moving forward without that person, but you'll
never know happiness until you walk away
from the person who ruins your peace of mind.
I believe that there is someone reading this now
who really needs these words, and so I hope that
person understands that the love they've been
longing for lives within their own heart and
eventually their efforts will be appreciated by
someone who is strong enough to care for their
heart. Be your own hero tonight; it's time to reach
for your own hand. I believe in your ability to
move forward, to move on.

harshest winter.

my mother dismissed me fairly young

my shoulders cold from a chilly Georgia air

the beginnings of a homelessness

that i had always felt

due to taking up spaces in places

where i felt i didn't belong

the wind took several shots at me

as i sat on the curb

not angry just hurt

too tired to say a word

too cold to register what had happened

the rest is all a blur

it was almost as if i blinked

and somehow there i was

18 with no home

living out of a raggedy suitcase

stuck in winter, not just the weather

but in the confines of my heart

September 7th 2018.

I wonder about you. There are nights where I
can't find sleep. There are nights where insomnia
drowns out whatever opportunity I had to find
rest. Those nights are the loudest, you know?
Those nights creep up on me without warning,
and I'm forced to lie there with a paralyzing sense
of concern. I wonder about you and how you're
doing. I think about you even when you feel like
the world has forgotten your name. I lie here
beneath the moon, drowned out by the silence of
heartache, thinking about you even when you feel
as though no one cares, but I do. There are nights
where my inability to find my dreams keeps me
lost in the endless nightmare of caring about
someone who no longer seems to care about
themselves. It is in these moments where the
night sky is the heaviest and the glow from the
moon is enough to blind crying eyes.

Have you lost yourself entirely? Do you even
remember who you were before those storms
erupted in your soul, forcing your heart to break
beneath the weight of the rain? Can you even
recall what it means or how it feels to be happy?
I think somewhere along the way, you lost sight
of everything you set out to look for, and maybe
you're just now waking up to the realization that
you've been gone for far too long. You've been
through it and so determined not to lose it that
you've closed your eyes in effort to ignore the
chaos that dwells beside you. You've suffered so
long that you've grown used to the abuse of the
world and the people who inhabit it. There is a
power, an ultimate strength that has always lived

deep beneath the surface of who you are, and yet somehow along the way, you lost the map to everything that could eventually set you free.

I wish the world wasn't so unkind to you; I wish "love" felt like bliss to you instead of something that would eventually cause you to break down. Nothing about this life has felt fair, and yet there were moments where you took it all in stride, refusing to give in or give up under the pressures of existing. Don't you remember the moments of feeling the ground beneath you break, giving way to pits of sadness, and still you fought to pull yourself out of that despair? The rain would intensify but you found ways to go untouched. And sure there have been times in your life where the emotional storms lasted way too long. There are days and nights that have felt too long, but even with your back against the wall, you fought.

Maybe these words won't mean much because we're strangers but the strangest thing is happening. I feel the need to reach for you, not in effort to save you but for the simple reason of reminding you how often you survived and pushed through hardship. I know you don't know me, I know we don't know each other, but we were brought together by both of our needs to overcome the storms that brew within the heart that is struggling to move forward with life.

all about you.

She is you, all powerful and capable of evolving
even when others wish to prevent you from
building up the courage to grow and let go. This
year has been tough, and yet here you are, still
standing, at times not knowing how much further
you'll be able to go, but here you are reading
these words. I don't think it's too late. Sure you've
spent some time in a relationship that drains your
spirit. You've spent many moments struggling
with letting go because your feelings were
always honest, you just fell for a liar who has
always been good at saying the right things while
proving to be incapable of making good on their
promises. They say sorry then continue to do the
things they apologize for. They claim to love you
even while they act as if they hate you.

You've come here in search of something that'll
keep you going. You've come here in search of
some version of hope, a reminder that things
will get better. Something written to help you
feel stronger. I can't pretend to know exactly
how you're feeling while reading this, but I will
say this to you . . . you'd have to be one hell of a
mighty woman to still be standing after all you've
been through, and I'm just the stranger who
cares. This is not about me. This was written for
and inspired by whoever needs it. I believe these
words will reach the right person. If you happen
to come upon these words in your moment of
need, then I've accomplished something, and if
for some reason this doesn't reach you, I'll keep
trying.

This is a sign, the one you said you wanted.
Whenever you feel down and out, whenever life
gets tough. Whenever your relationship tears you
down, read these words and remember that you
are evolving. You are becoming stronger and you
will outgrow anything that no longer deserves
a space in your life. To the woman reading this,
suffering from frustration and heartache, tired of
being taken for granted by the person who should
have always appreciated her. It's time to choose
yourself. I know it's easier said than done, but you
are capable!

which one is he.

There are two types of men in this world, the ones who will stay and the ones who will leave. The ones who will know exactly what they have when they have you and the ones who have to lose you to know your value. There are two types of men in this world and you more than likely are familiar with the guy who tells you lies in hopes of making you fall in love alone. That guy will always tell you what you want to hear and yet continue to do the opposite.

There are two types of guys in this world, and I hope after all you've been through, that you find someone who will match your effort and not only say the right things but do the right things. My hope for you is that you find the someone who has been searching for you all this time. There is nothing romantic about a person who has to lose you in order to understand the magnitude of your existence.

Your heart is way too valuable to be placed back into the hands of the person who left you to entertain someone else. You are not a second option and you are not an afterthought. I hope these words reach the person who needs them the most, and I hope that person never forgets that in a night sky, their heart is the moon. In a world filled with chaos, your soul is peace and you deserve to be with someone who knows exactly how beautiful and profound it is to be loved by someone like you. I'm writing to you because maybe you're tired, maybe you're at the end of your rope, maybe you're so close to giving in, please don't.

I am grateful for this opportunity to speak to you in this moment and hopefully these words will help encourage you to move forward with your life. It's time to choose yourself and let go of the person who has chosen to hurt your heart.

you are profound.

I understand that there are moments where
you feel like you're not good enough, there are
times where you feel a mess. There are moments
where you suffer in silence and your heart breaks
beneath a midnight moon. I understand that
you're imperfect and sometimes your flaws are
loud like glass smashing against the pavement,
and even with all of that, you somehow find a
way to survive the night. You always find a way
to pick yourself up, you always find a way to
shine through the night sky like shooting stars.
There will be moments where you feel like falling
or giving up, but you must remember the magic
that lives deep within your heart and beneath
your bones. You must not forget to be kind to
your heart, even when others fail to appreciate
you, and you must remember to always choose
yourself even when the person you care about
refuses to. YOU ARE CAPABLE, YOU ARE
MIGHTY, YOU ARE PROFOUND AND
IMPORTANT. So, to all the women reading this,
I just want to say thank you for being strong. You,
tonight, have inspired these words. Right now,
this belongs to you.

what it feels like.

Right now your heart aches in the wake of a
restless night. You'll struggle to sleep and so your
pain will bring you here to these words. I know
it feels like the world around you is crumbling
and the foundation beneath your feet is breaking,
but women like you learn to fly when there's
no ground to walk on, and so in this moment,
that's what you'll do. You fight because you're a
warrior. You survive because you're magic. It's
time to choose yourself, it's time to reach for your
own hand. And if you should ever forget about
how powerful you are, just read this again, I'll be
here to remind you. Go into the night, not with
fear but with courage, because you are a torch
and you will light your own path to freedom.

a witness.

I watched it happen, I witnessed her fall in a love
that would later become a downfall, a regret. I bet
she's reading this now, weary and broken. Too
tired to focus on moving on, afraid of starting
over. Pretending to be okay, forcing a fake smile.
Laughing to keep from crying. Maybe she'll
ignore this, but even then, I know she's reading
this now. Tired of the words that lead to no action.
Tired of promises that were always empty. Trying
to fill a void with an empty lover who will never
love her and even though most of the love she's
known has left her undone. She still matters,
you matter, and you just want to be treated the
way you treat others. You just want an effort
that mirrors your own and I hope you read these
words.

You always break down, and every so often,
you fall beneath the hand of someone who has
never deserved to touch you, let alone hurt
you. You find yourself forgiving people who
were never sorry, forgiving people who never
intended to apologize, and even if they do, it's
usually followed by the fact you discovered
their wrongdoing on your own, everything they
would have never told you in the first place, but
all those nights of falling apart and obsessing
over what they're actually doing somehow pay
off, or at least you feel like they do. You find
yourself apologizing even when you're not wrong.
Apologizing in an effort to keep a person who
no longer deserves to be a part of your life. You
apologize because for some odd reason you're
made to feel guilty for expressing your sadness
when hurt or expressing your doubt when lied to.

You always break down beneath the night sky
like the one that sits outside your window at
this very moment. You find yourself attempting
to piece together the shards of your heart.
Struggling through the darkness with no light,
in search of the pieces that will make you feel
complete.

Even with all of this, even in the midst of
suffering. Even in the moments where you
lose your footing. You survive, you always do.
You're the soul that has learned to conquer any
and everything that attempts to destroy you.
Somehow, each night, beneath this very moon.
You find new ways to make it through the night
and this is why I'm writing about you.

a loss, September 7th 2018.

i apologize to the broken hearts

that belong to those who feel like

they can no longer go on

my condolences to all the lives

that have been lost under the weight of sadness

we are so strong

and yet we are all so fragile

beneath it all

fighting to survive

struggling to live

you are not alone

forgiveness, hope.

victim of a broken home

and a chaotic childhood

your father absent

your mother barely tried

searching for love among wolves

liars and cheats

incapable of recognizing truth

because your family was rarely honest

and so i tried to be someone you never had

i tried to give you something

you never knew

and you decided to throw it away

you weren't ready

and so i forgive you

for choosing someone

who offered something familiar

and i forgive you

because it's not your fault

pushing me away out of fear

i guess i was trying to teach you

how to love yourself

but i could never reach you

and so i hope you learn

to reach for yourself

i hope you figure out

that you deserve so much more

than what you were given

before, 2013.

i say goodbye
but it never takes
my confidence breaks
beneath the weight of fear

the fear of starting over
without the person
i thought i needed

but deception and resentment
have overrun this place
and you no longer feel like home

i'm too tired to tolerate you
and yet at the same time
too tired to pick up my shit
and leave

i believed in you like religion

but here i am losing faith

and it's going to take a miracle

for me to get over this

but i know i can

because the heart of someone like me

isn't meant to be held

by harmful hands like yours

at times, we're wrong.

it's just that sometimes
the heart falls for the wrong person
and sometimes the heart
only realizes this
while it shatters across the floors
of a place that used to feel like home

and i know those moments
can feel like the hardest thing
you've faced

but even while broken
and even while the world around you
no longer feels safe

i think the heart finds a way
to rediscover itself, piece itself back together
and it learns to love again
when the time is right

so, yes, you're going to love

the wrong people

but that's just so

you'll know the difference

between what is real and what isn't

when you're depressed
the brightest day seems dark

and the sound of laughter
screams like a banshee

soul warning.

beware of men in masks

making promises to your heart

that they have no intention of keeping

telling you everything you want to hear

with no action to follow

using you as a stepping-stone

to fulfill their deepest desires

beware of men in masks

hiding in plain sight

afraid that if you see their faces

you'll see a half truth or a whole lie

search for her.

she took a pen

filled with her tears

and wrote the words

"please find me"

on an old piece of paper

and tossed it out into the night sky

survive this day.

sometimes my highs feel low

and my mornings

are without the sun

yet somehow i rise

even with a broken wing

because sometimes you have to go

even when you feel like giving up

to my Samantha, 722.

my heaven on earth

rests between your shoulders

somewhere inside your arms

right below your chin

near your heart

you hold me

and the sadness leaves

you hold me

and i remember

that heaven lies beside me

in this home, in this room

in this bed

heaven is you

at the start, 722.

we ate slices of pizza

because we were too broke

to eat something better

pretending to be satisfied

with what we chose to consume

because our options were nearly obsolete

we'd lie in bed

cramping both of our large personalities

in that small room that you were renting

before i even entered your life

but you allowed me to share that space

and for the brief time of occupying those four
walls together

we made a home

we made love

we made each other laugh and sometimes cry

and then we made it out of there

but the memory of eating slices of pizza

on that full-size bed with that small AC unit

in the window

will always be beautiful

because we shared those moments together

lucky me, us.

you were my lucky accident

the stranger

who gave me strange feelings

my savior in the night

an anonymous letter

that i had to read

you came for me

like a melody

that was stuck in my head

a song without a name

until you named it after us

_____

write a love letter to yourself

and in the letter

make promises to give your heart

everything that others denied you of receiving

———————

shackle me down

lock me in love

i don't mind

i'll never wish

to be free from you

young and old.

young heart

old soul

at an age

where people ignore you

and what you're feeling

an age where you feel so much

of what you struggle to explain

but you need to be heard

there's a story living inside you

that should be told

don't let them silence you

don't let them muffle

your emotional screams

a phoenix.

the pain didn't break her

she took the heartache

and transformed her scars

into a representation of power

unafraid of flames

unbothered by the heat

she became like fire

she torched the devil

one hell of a woman

romanticize yourself

because here and now

you are a lonesome

beautiful love story

waiting to be told

and heard by the right ears

romanticize yourself

because you are love

woman, set free.

she broke like waves
eager to kiss the shore
she broke like chains
chasing her freedom

the heart, a journey.

true love is finding someone
you'll never be prepared to lose
but deciding to stay
loving, living, and waiting to the end

running from the past
trying to extend the present
and fearful of a future
where you'll have to survive
without them in your life

and though that seems tough
it's heartbreaking to think about

i believe the lucky ones are the souls
who find each other in this lifetime
and die knowing what it meant
to truly mean something to someone

———————————

your heart is too beautiful

for the chaos it has endured

and so i hope you get what you need

i hope you get what you deserve

1:11am.

those empty bottles are filled with stories
of a lonesome heart, falling toward the moon
in search of more, in search of peace

you reach out into the middle of the night
hoping for answers, wishing on stars
whispering to the moon
eager to open up
with this overwhelming desire
to be heard

and maybe the pages in this book
are the ears that are worthy
of hearing your story
and maybe fate brought you here
maybe the universe knows
that your soul needed something
to get you through the night

maybe this is it

Dear you, the broken girl I wrote this for. The broken girl who struggled through womanhood, the weary soul who could always find her voice through writing. The one with the bruises from past loves and heartaches. The one who no matter what stood in your way, you found the courage to keep going. I'm sorry that your mother left you without lessons and so you had to figure it all out on your own. I'm sorry that your father was incapable of being the man you needed him to be and so you found yourself searching for love in the hands of wolves pretending to give a damn about you. To the woman who fought when giving up seemed easier, to the soul of the woman who transformed her pain into magic. I fell in love with you, even when you thought you were unworthy of love. I fell in love with you and your imperfections. I saw your scars and still called you beautiful. I heard the pain in your voice, and my name rolling off your tongue was a melody I had longed to hear, and now we're here, together. My heart kept safe in your hands as I guard yours. I'm sorry for all the times that I wasn't there to cheer you on or to remind you of how special you've always been. I love you so much and I thank the heavens each and every day for lending you the strength to fight through the pain. This was entirely inspired by you, my soul mate. The keeper of my dreams, you are the only poem that I'll ever need to read.

———————

a love that feels real
a love that doesn't hurt
a relationship filled with truth
a relationship filled with effort

this is all she ever wanted
this was all she ever thought about
while tears rolled down her face
painting her skin the color blue

glass full, empty.

sitting still
like water in a short glass
full but never enough

i am nearly overflowing
with a love you
refuse to appreciate

wondering why
you drink from others
yet never from me

how i can be so full
of a love deserving of more
and still made to feel empty

by someone who claims
to thirst for something real
but refuses to choose my glass

"Burn his mask," I told her.

"Set his lies on fire."

born from fire, she danced with flames

with a power that shook the devil's domain

_____

you can be strong
and still feel weak
you can love someone
and still feel the need to leave

you know they're no longer
good for your soul
and still it can be hard to let go
you've been stuck between
wanting to be loved
and wanting to feel nothing

all of this because you've fallen
for someone incapable
of loving you the way you deserve
and this has been your struggle

i thought

you were freedom

but it turns out

that you were just a prison

disguised as home

there are no exits here

and so i decided to make one

it's been hard to walk away

and so i decided to run

to new beginnings.

you are the disaster

that only lives in my yesterdays

the trouble from my troubling past

you are a sorrowful storm

a broken, out-of-tune melody

a song full of lies

i fooled myself

into believing

you could fall for me

there were dark clouds

hovering above my head

always too high

for me to notice

and it took years of torment

to finally figure out

that my love was much bigger

than your hate

i survived your lies

and created a new fate

the mask.

What's behind that mask? She asked, he didn't
reply. The sigh from her heart could be heard
from the distance of time it took to heal from
the disappointment of loving the wrong person,
and the confusion she wore, turned her face to
sadness.

He was hiding and she was tired of the muffled
"I love you" from a face with no expression, a
face she couldn't see, and so one night while he
slept, she took both hands and gently removed
his mask, and not a word came from her lips as
she sat calmly on the bed. She managed to put
his mask back on, and by morning he awoke to a
letter on her pillow, her side of the bed void of her
body.

The letter read, "Now I know why you wear
a mask. You were afraid that I'd see you for
who you always were, a lie within a lie. A man
promising to give me everything, and yet here I
am, feeling like nothing."

crowded minds.

i hate crowds

they're too noisy for my soul

the voices sting like hornets

to an eardrum

the close proximity to others

in this city

is enough to drain you

of all your energy

and so you find yourself

wanting to find a corner of the world

that isn't occupied by many people

or better yet, no one at all

you recharge by being alone

noise drowned out by silence

solitude conjures peace

she, the revolution.

she spoke and there was

a revolution in her voice

she was not only the type

of woman to be feared

but she was also

the type of woman to follow

her powerful disruptive

and profound presence

could bring kings to their knees

her powerful nature

made her a natural-born leader

the strength in her soul

kept her prepared for war

———————

beaten down by neglect

overwhelmed with sadness

i no longer know what to say

i have no more fight left for us

i've retreated into shade

hidden away by darkness

the words won't come out

and so silence is my song

Where did I lose you, where did it go? It being
my own soul, my own essence. The very thing
that I thought I could never live without. How
does a person go on without themselves? Staring
into mirrors with no reflection. Walking down
streets under moonlight without a shadow,
breathing in cold air but exhaling nothing. I feel
nothing and everything all at once. Twice a day
gray clouds rain down upon me without pity.
When did I lose you, where did I go?

Promise me this. When your heart feels like
it can't go on and your soul begins to struggle
beneath the weight of it all. Promise me you'll
reach for anything that will calm the hurricanes
beating at your chest. Promise me you'll reach
for the words of someone who can speak to
the darkness that plagues your mind. Some
Samantha King Holmes when your nights grow
so overwhelming that the night skies attempt to
swallow you whole or maybe the words of R.M.
Drake for the midnights or the hours before
sunrise where you struggle to find rest. There is
healing in the words of writers who know pain
best. There is sanctuary on pages of writers who
know exactly what it means to fall like you, to
fight like you. To survive like you. Promise me
that you won't let the struggle of what you're
facing keep you from the victory that is meant
to be yours. I know that these are just words on
a page and I know I'm just some stranger who
has your attention, but I need you to believe in
the idea that you are capable of finding your way
through this dark phase in your life and I want
you to know that you are not alone. There will be
others who will stumble upon these words, this
page, in search of solace. In search for clarity and
I just hope that I can be of some assistance. Read
these words until you understand that there is a
power that lives within you and a will that can
never be broken.

oh dear girl

you don't need a man

to feel like a woman

you don't need a king

to feel royal

in this book.

The heart of an angel breaks in the hands of a
coward. A lover incapable of loving you and
so your smile is broken and your peace gets
interrupted. Your soul almost feels as if it's been
ruptured. You've been losing your mind, driven
crazy by someone who claimed to care, and yet
when you look up, they are never there.

You keep thinking to yourself, how many times
must I fall? Stuck receiving nothing while always
giving your all. I ache beside you, a stranger in
the chair next to yours. Wishing I could speak
to you but my voice gets drowned out by sounds
of sadness and so I write it down. Hoping you'll
read this, hoping you'll find this page. My
sentiments and well wishes for you, in this book.

after the ending, begin.

I was young, 16, when I met the person who
would destroy me later. My head in the clouds
and my eyes blinded by what I believed to be
love and so no wonder I couldn't see the hatred
following me like my own shadow. Living with
me, looking me in the eyes this whole time.
Something was wrong, and though it stood
before me in plain sight, it felt right. I was wrong,
forcing a puzzle piece into a space it could
never fit. Holding on when I should have let go,
knowing there was no benefit. I lost an entire
decade on an idea of love that felt more like hell,
but in the end, I learned three major lessons. That
true love begins from within, and self-love will
keep the heart from falling into the wrong hands,
and life doesn't end with a relationship with
someone who never deserved your love in the
first place.

I learned that in order to begin the process of
falling in love with the right person, you must
first learn to walk away from anyone who proves
to be the wrong fit for your future.

———————————

vanity

killed

the

poet

vanity

ruined

the meaning

behind

the words

vanity

destroyed

the art

we rise

like overflowing

rivers

we fight

under attack

overwhelmed

by heartache

refusing to quit

struggling to survive

deciding to live

i hope we get there

to a place of peace

a moment of victory

a lifetime of joy

the world dealt you shit

but your grit

keeps you alive

you are a moment

of truth

in a sea of lies

fighting to stay afloat

swimming against the current

determined not to drown

bound for glory

bound for love

you never let

yourself down

———————————

i used to fear

running out of words

but lately

i fear running out of space

searching for a place

to leave my thoughts

somewhere visible

for you to read

i used to think

i'd run out of things to say

or that the ink would run dry

i'd die happy

knowing this reached you

poems to teach you

how to keep fighting

and to never let sadness

defeat you

and never let misery keep you

_____

i used to fear

running out of words

but lately

i fear running out of time

running on empty

a loss of the energy needed

to reach my hands out to you

searching for a place

to leave my thoughts

somewhere safe

somewhere tucked away

in a place

where your eyes can follow

poetry that heals you

poetry that reveals you

to more than you

could ever imagine

keep fighting

and never let misery

keep you

you never know

just how important

your childhood is

until you've lost it

beneath the weight

of adulthood

_____

cry

empty yourself

of feelings

that no longer

deserve to be felt

cry

until you are free

oh the nights

i wasted on you

using whiskey

to bury my memory

of us

staring into the moon

for answers

to questions

i was too afraid

to ask out loud

consumed by the silence

of the void

i was trying to fill

desperate to feel

something other than pain

struggling to free

myself from you

those nights broke me

and yet made me stronger

who knew the heart

could rain

thunder forming

within the soul

but storms teach us

how to be stronger

we all have cloudy skies

to overcome

_____

she raged peacefully

she raged beautifully

10/25/18.

They're so nice to everyone but you. So often that very thought plagues your mind and causes havoc in your heart. You give so much of yourself. The effort, the energy. All wasted on someone who will never appreciate the amount of consideration you have for them, and even though it hurts, you keep trying out of love. You hate the way this feels, and still you keep trying because deep down you hope that doing more will make a difference, but it won't. I hope you find someone who wants to see you smile, someone who wants you to be happy. Someone who will do whatever it takes to make you feel a peace of mind. I hope you find the person who fits directly into your idea of what true love means. It can be a lonely, dark space, being in love alone, but I hope you find the courage to set yourself free.

to be Frank.

I used to ask myself, how could someone like
you ever love someone incapable of loving you
back? How could someone with a heart like
yours ever find itself in the hands of someone
who never deserved to hold it? I used to stay up
late at night staring at the ceiling, you know the
one in that small town, in that small room. That
small room we shared before the high-rises called
our names. That ceiling with the water damage
and stained walls. I used to lie there in complete
confusion, losing sleep wondering how you
could ever believe in all those illusions of love.
Lies told by men who were never man enough to
care for you in the way you deserved. Then one
day I listened as you asked your father questions
he refused to answer and any reply he offered
was soaked in lies. There was another day when
you needed a favor, some help, and his response
struck a sort of disappointment in your soul and
not to mention your stories of how he and your
mother let you and your siblings go. The first year
was tough, our first year living together under a
weak roof. Cracked foundation and old chipped
paint walls. This is where you lived before I
entered the picture and this was the picture your
"family" allowed you to frame, I guess. This is
where you lived when we met and that little room
was now our home as I often asked myself: if
your father loved you like you claimed he did,
then how could he allow his youngest to occupy
an old home built upon tainted soil? Out of love,
I got my shit together while he sang the same old
song, a broken melody, a deadbeat. I got my shit
together out of love for you, for us. The desire

to strive for something more, birthed by the
love and admiration I have for you. We got our
shit together on our own. We gathered our shit
together, packed boxes, stuffed bags, and set out
on a new adventure. I used to ask myself how
I could have missed you, my view obstructed
by people incapable of loving me. Your energy
invested in the wrong people because of a void
left by parents who couldn't parent. I used to
ask myself how you could ever love a man who
lets you down, but then I began to realize that
the answer was there all along at family dinners
and holiday get-togethers. The answer to all my
questions was looking me in the eye or, come
to think of it, he rarely looked me in the eyes.
The shame, the guilt, the delusion, and the lies.
I used to ask myself how you could ever let your
effort go to waste, but then I witnessed you try
harder for someone who rarely tried at all. It gets
worse, you know? I could go on and on about the
missteps and miscues and the moments you feel
like he forgets you.

The other night he used words he should have
never used in a tone that was unacceptable. He
said things that shook my soul but made you cry,
and this is where I draw the line, and yet I used
to ask myself all the time. How could someone
like you find your mind in shambles and your
heart in a pit and now I know that he was part of
the reason for most of that shit. He didn't leave
completely but he was there enough. I know
this because instead of depending on him, you
ventured out into chaos in search of love. A
love that you knew nothing about because the
people who should have loved you enough to

keep you safe chose to leave you out . . . in the wilderness where wolves pace back and forth in search of prey. A child with enough courage to take risks but not old enough to understand the consequences of being a daughter to a mother and father who couldn't be what you needed most. You were reaching for the stars, and they should have been the clouds, yet they caused the rain. Forcing you to struggle through the storm but that wasn't your fault and it still isn't. I can recall that one Thanksgiving where he seemed ungrateful or the Christmas where he entered our loving home seeming hateful. Your father taught you to settle for less, but you had the courage to give someone like me a chance. Someone different with something different to offer. Someone who could never treat his daughters the way your father has treated you.

I marvel at you, Samantha, the way you smile when tears could be expected. The way you still strive for love even in moments when others force you to feel neglected, and I want you to know that with me, you will always be protected, and I'm sorry that your heart has gone through so much pain when all someone like you has ever deserved was someone to love you completely, even in moments where you felt like you weren't good enough, and I'd like to be that for you. I used to concern myself with the way others failed you, but now I realize that I must focus on being the type of person who deserves to be loved by someone like you.

———————————

My dear Samantha, thank you for surviving

thank you for always being so brave

the landing index.

1:11am.   191
10/25/18.   223
after the ending, begin.   209
all about you.   160
all that was left   146
a long life   138
a loss, September 7th 2018.   168
a love that feels real   193
a phoenix.   186
at the start, 722.   180
at times, we're wrong.   173
a witness.   166
beaten down by neglect   204
before, 2013.   171
born from fire, she danced with flames   196
"Burn his mask," I told her.   195
but darling   151
corners.   132
crowded minds.   202
cry   218
Dear you, the broken girl I wrote this for.   192
far and near.   129
forgiveness, hope.   169
glass full, empty.   194
harshest winter.   157
her hands could hold a hurricane   150
i can't sleep   134

in Manhattan.   128
in this book.   208
it begins I.   119
it begins II.   124
i thought   198
i too shatter easily   147
it rarely ends.   120
i used to fear   213
i used to fear   215
journeying through life   127
losing a queen.   155
lucky me, us.   182
maybe she was tired   130
muscle memory.   122
My dear Samantha, thank you
  for surviving   227
my dreams are in black and white   135
my hesitance is a remnant   141
no one knows   142
oh dear girl   207
oh the nights   219
overcome, again.   121
please.   139
Promise me this.   206
romanticize yourself   187
search for her.   177
Selene.   131
September 1st 2018.   156
September 7th 2018.   158
shackle me down   184
she moved like the flame   152
she raged peacefully   222
she, the revolution.   203
sometimes i avoid mirrors   144

sometimes i wish the heart   153
soul warning.   176
starting over   154
survive this day   178
terrible, remember.   148
that overpowering desire   133
the bombs are dropping in my heart   137
the heart, a journey.   189
the mask.   201
the pictures capture the lies so well   136
there are nights where i shout prayers   149
the world dealt you shit   212
This is a sign, the one you said you wanted.   161
time wasted.   145
to be Frank.   224
to my Samantha, 722.   179
to new beginnings.   199
vanity   210
we rise   211
what it feels like.   165
what will happen.   125
when you're depressed   175
Where did I lose you, where did it go?   205
which one is he.   162
who knew the heart   221
woman, set free.   188
write a love letter to yourself   183
*You always break down, and every so
  often, you fall beneath the hand of
  someone who has never deserved to
  touch you, let alone hurt you.*   167
you are profound.   164
you can be strong   197
you feel broken   143

the landing   231

you never know   217
young and old.   185
your heart is too beautiful   190
you spend all your life looking for love   126

FALLING TOWARD *the* MOON

Andrews McMeel Publishing
a division of Andrews McMeel Universal
1130 Walnut Street, Kansas City, Missouri 64106

www.andrewsmcmeel.com

20 21 22 23 24 BVG 10 9 8 7 6 5 4 3 2

ISBN: 978-1-5248-5383-9

Library of Congress Control Number: 2019941123

Editor: Patty Rice
Art Director/Designer: Diane Marsh
Production Editor: Amy Strassner
Production Manager: Cliff Koehler

Cover illustration by Hannah Olson

ATTENTION: SCHOOLS AND BUSINESSES
Andrews McMeel books are available at quantity
discounts with bulk purchase for educational,
business, or sales promotional use. For information,
please e-mail the Andrews McMeel Publishing Special
Sales Department: specialsales@amuniversal.com.